WINNING
BATTLE
THE
AGAINST MYSELF
Overcoming the Way Things Are

ANDREWS R. SMITH

AuthorHouse™
1663 Liberty Drive
Bloomington, IN 47403
www.authorhouse.com
Phone: 1-800-839-8640

Published by AuthorHouse 2/26/2013

ISBN: 978-1-4208-4880-9 (sc)
ISBN: 978-1-4634-9111-6 (e)

Any people depicted in stock imagery provided by Thinkstock are
models, and such images are being used for illustrative purposes only.
Certain stock imagery © Thinkstock.

This book is printed on acid-free paper.

Because of the dynamic nature of the Internet, any web
addresses or links contained in this book may have changed
since publication and may no longer be valid.

The views expressed in this work are solely those of the author
and do not necessarily reflect the views of the publisher, and
the publisher hereby disclaims any responsibility for them.

Table of Contents

Before you attempt to fight the war,
you must first win the battle.

Introduction

God warned me and said, "If you don't establish a Reality of my Presence that surpasses all realities of life, you will lose my presence and be lost because you will be consumed by the realities of this world". I know many of you are probably wondering what that means? In this life, there are many things that are considered to be real. Some of those things include our jobs, our bills, our families, our struggles, our disappointments, our past, our personal agendas and our future. But in reality, what's real is not what the mind perceives, because some things are real whether we believe them or not. So, what is real?

Life provides many questions, but sometimes not enough answers. You will find that the answers to many of your questions are found within yourself. But, with you being your worst enemy, they may be difficult to find. It's time to stop seeking answers from the wrong people and start seeking God. I've fought many wars and lost many battles just because I've failed to realize what was real. But now, I've realized that before I begin to fight the war, I must learn to win the battle against myself.

Chapter One
Getting personal with God

At this point in my life it seems as though God has abandoned my ship. All of His great splendor which makes Him God is gone, vanished from my life forever. Although I know better, it still feels that way. We all come to a point in our lives in which the presence of God seems to have left our temples. With Him out of our temples, we feel an inability to praise or worship Him. So, we call on those whom we feel can get a prayer through to aid us in our time of separation. We fail to understand that God hears our every word and sees our every

Andrews R. Smith

tear. We are very similar to cavemen when we feel absent from God. We care less sometimes about our attire, we pay less attention to hygiene, we allow our hair and facial hair to become less attractive, and we love to dwell in dark, small and lonely places. When I want to be alone, I sometimes go into the bathroom, turn off the lights and lie down on the floor. I know you're probably saying, "he's not absent from God, he's nuts!" Yeah, that's what I thought too, but it was comfortable and soothing to me. Whether we want to admit it or not, we all have some sort of craziness in us. Now, whether it's enough to receive a check from the government is another question. God allowed me to see what I was doing when I closed myself up in my bathroom. When the pressures of life come crashing down upon our individual worlds, we run to find shelter. My shelter was the bathroom. The closed door followed by the turning off of the lights gave me the access to escape, while the lying down on the floor made my escape comfortable. When

God showed me this, it completely blew my mind. I was completely comfortable in my escape away from the pressures that were upon me. We must be very careful in the things that we do to escape our problems. Some of us drink, do drugs, party all the time, live promiscuous lives or are in denial. Be careful, because if it feels comfortable, you may just get lost there. A fantasy world is no place to live. Although it may be fun, you may forget how to find your way back home. We must learn to face our problems and not let the devil sell us the "feel good" line. Satan tell us, "If it feels good, it must be good". This is the tactic that was used on Eve, in the book of Genesis 3: 16. When Eve saw that the fruit was good for food and pleasing to the eye, she felt compelled to taste it. My friends always told me that "there is nothing wrong with looking". Although they were referring to something quite different from fruit, the result is still the same. We fail to understand that elongated looking takes a snapshot of the item and stores it into our memory banks for future retrieving. You may not do anything at that particular moment, but there will be a moment in which time is available and strength is not, when the image of your snapshot will reappear. Since time is on your side and you are at a point of vulnerability, you have all day to indulge in that "sin" which separates you from God. The enemy Satan allows the sins to "feel good" to keep us coming back for more. We must ask ourselves, does feeling good come before obedience to God? Because if it does, we will be too busy trying to find pleasure instead of doing the will of God. And if we can't or don't do the will of our Father, then the ministry of our lives will be useless. Our lives should be living proof that God exists. If no one can see Christ in your life, it makes you wonder what your life would become without Christ? Not much of anything.

Chapter Two
Up Against the family

There was a time in which I forsook God for the benefit of family. I thought that's what God wanted me to do. I thought He wanted me to provide, nurture, educate and lead my family, but I was wrong. I wasn't wrong about the providing, nurturing, educating and leading, but I was wrong about putting them first. Before you chop off my head and put it on a broomstick to scare off crows, let me explain. I was taught from the early church that family comes first. Being ignorant of the statement, I felt as long as my family was doing fine, then God must be pleased with me. Wrong! God is a jealous God and wants no other god before Him (Exodus 20:4) Whether we know it or not, we set people and things up to be gods. Not that we do it intentionally, but it happens. When we set people or things up as gods, God our Father becomes jealous. Look at it this way. Say for example, you bring a child into this world. You clothe her in the best that you can provide, you feed her when she's hungry and you also give her gifts just because she's your daughter. But when she gets older, instead of spending most of her time with you, the person who was always there for her, she spends most of her time with her aunt, someone who only comes around on holidays. Ouch!!! That's gotta hurt! Well, how do you think God feels when we put our families before Him. If it weren't for His breath, we wouldn't have a family to enjoy. Understand, I'm not telling you to drop your family obligations and join the neighborhood monastery, although that may sound good to some of you. I'm just concerned about the strain that could be placed upon an individual who doesn't know the importance of prioritizing and having a true relationship with Jesus.

Many, many years ago I was in full-time mode, father, husband, business owner, student and friend. When I went back and thought about it, I was crazy, full-time! You may look at that and say, "I don't see anything wrong with that picture". But, if you take a closer look, you will notice that everyone got a piece of me but God. Everything that involved the welfare of my family took priority over anything else.

Some people act like pigs, the hog everything and everybody for themselves. God was in fact not pleased with me. When I felt God tugging at me for attention, I didn't know what to do. First, I started ignoring Him because I knew I was in the wrong. Then later things started to crumble all around me. My petition to seek a final grant in order to graduate with a Bachelor degree Healthcare Operations was denied, the business which I worked so hard to build starting failing and my marriage dissolved in divorce. Everything that was anything to my family's benefit was gone, including my family. I firmly believe that God has a way of getting our attention. (Praise God!) Never put anything before God unless you're willing to lose it. Now, after I've finally gotten the picture, things have changed. After almost three years of an abstinent lifestyle, God brought before me a woman. I made absolutely sure that she was from God. I wanted to see her birth certificate, shot records, social security card and her driver's license. Before her, God chose me to be one of His disciples. I didn't accept at first, but later I did. We were married and enjoyed each other along with the presence of God. She's a very spiritual woman and loves to worship God. I told God that I wasn't going to date anyone, but the woman He would give to me. And that's the way it happened. Trying to learn from past experiences, I now put God first in everything I do. When I put my family first, everything crumbled. But now, I put Him first, and not only do I feel His presence, but I see His hand moving in my life. I feel as though I'm sitting on the back of a turtle who is walking toward my box of blessings. Sometimes I want to just jump off the back of that turtle and run to that box of blessings myself, at least I'll get there faster. Then, there are times when I'm patient, but my family wants to jump off toward the box. It's often difficult to be patient in an impatient world. God's timing is not like ours. He wants to purge us into that perfect vessel He knows we can become. That's why it's very important to have a family which is "God conscious".

When a family is "God conscious", the blessings that we receive will come easier and faster. There will be less confusion and fewer headaches. God's purpose for us to have children is to tell them about Him, so that there will be more glory, more praise and more worship of Him who created us. When a family is not "God conscious", there is plenty of room for the enemy (Satan) to intervene. In the Bible book of Matthew 12:25, Jesus says that a house that's divided against itself will fall. That verse of scripture is very important to me and should be to you. Jesus is saying that those who live together under the same roof, sharing beds, food and space should be able to live in peace and with the intention of making things better. But those of you who live under the same roof, but not sharing anything and not trying to make anything work, will cause their home to be destroyed. Those of you who are leaders in the home, don't allow family to dictate your relationship with God. Instead, communicate with them, including the children, so that God will get the glory not just in your life, but in the lives of your family members. Satan loves to use our spouses and children against us to get us off focus, so be aware.

Chapter Three
Who Are My Friends

When I was growing up, I had a lot of people who considered themselves my friends, and vice versa. I thought maybe it was because I danced in a group which performed at talent shows across the city. People love to attach themselves to others in the spotlight. The attachment derives from the need for attention. Everyone wants attention, but some more than others. Some people go through great lengths to receive attention. They jump off buildings to their deaths, they perform crazy out of the ordinary stunts or they lie to make themselves greater than who they are. They do a number of things. One way for me to know who my friend is, is when I'm in need. Most people are with you until you need something from them. When you need something from them, they tend to make themselves scarce. Well, you don't need to be a "rocket scientist" to figure this one out. Leave 'em. Whether we admit it or not our friends are the ones who help mold us into what we are today. That's why it's very important to seek those individuals who are going in the same direction that you are going in. Since we spend so much time with our friends, they tend to have such a great influence on our lives. They talk us into doing things we should do and they talk us out of doing things we shouldn't do. I was riding with a friend in his car, when suddenly we hit another car. My friend failed to see if the other lane was clear before he passed to the other lane, and because he failed to look we hit the car. No one was hurt, but both cars were damaged. My friend told me that he didn't have his license with him and that they would take him to jail. So, because I did not want to see him go to jail, I took the ticket for him. As you would know, my friend was filled with joy that I did that for him. When you do things for a friend, there shouldn't be any doubt in your mind that your friend would do the same thing for you. I wasn't thinking about that at the time because I knew that I would never drive without my license, "typical teen-aged thinking". Needless to say, my friend lied to me about his license and about paying for the cost of the ticket. I ended up paying the ticket and almost paying for the damage to the other car. Teen-agers make sure your friend has a license to drive and has it with him/her at the time he/she is driving. Rule to live by.

In the Bible book of John 15:14, Jesus says, " you are my friends if you do what I command". So many have taken this verse out of its context. Boys tell their girlfriends to do certain things that the girls are not comfortable doing. They tell them that if they love them they will do it.

This kind of ultimatum puts a great deal of pressure on someone and should not be forced on a person if you love that person. This ultimatum makes one decide between two displeasing answers. If she says "yes", then she would have to do something that makes her uncomfortable. But, if she says "no", she takes the risk of losing someone she loves. Well, what do you do? Look at it this way, you must do what is right for you. If you don't know what's right for you, think, "what would Jesus do?" Would He sacrifice His life for the sake of others? Yes, but not that way. If you have to do something that would be displeasing to God, then the answer is "no". I don't care what the situation is or who the person is, "if you are not with Christ, then you are against Him".

Love consists of a two-way loyalty. When you give something in love, it will also return to you in love. I hear people say all the time that they do things for the sake of others that they love, even if the things that are done are against God. Let me put it to you plain and simple, there is no one on the face of this earth that is worth displeasing God for. I mean no one. Forget the four year old syndrome of pleasing someone you love and start thinking about pleasing someone who loves you. Get out of that pity party, because there's no one dancing. If you want to know who your friends are, look around you and find the ones who have been there for you through thick and thin. If you can't find anyone, start obeying the word of God, Jesus said, "He would be your friend". (John 15:14)

Chapter Four
Happily Ever After

After 2 divorces, I was about finished with the idea of having a soul mate and living happily ever after as they say in the books and movies. Relationships are hard and the idea of finding someone who will accept me and all of my faults makes the concept even harder to believe in. With brokenness in my bones, shame in my heart and doubt in my mind, I was ready and willing to cast out any thought that God could and will bring me the desires of my heart. Who is God? What is he doing up there? Does he even see me? Does he even care about what I'm going through? Who made him God over everything anyway? With all of that anger, doubt, frustration and fear inside of me, it was almost impossible to move beyond my struggles. How can a loving God allow bad things to happen? I kind of blame God for all of the things that happened to me. He was part of the blame for my 2 divorces, my ridiculous paycheck, the holes in my clothes and the just recently disconnection of my utilities! I felt all alone and was really beginning to not care about anything or anybody, I finally hit bottom, I was lonely and I felt alone.

After a long long time of being in despair, I've learned something very valuable. During those loneliest times of my life, I've learned that loneliness and feeling alone are 2 separate things. Wow!!! God really ministered to me during that time because I finally stop blaming Him for the decisions that I willfully and consciously made, without his advice or His directions for my life. When I begin to be honest with myself, I came to the conclusion that God had been talking with me all of the time, trying to counsel me every time I had a decision to make. He was telling me, "no, don't do that" or "yes, do that". I could not believe that the Creator of the universe was actually taking time out of His busy schedule to talk to little old me, but he was. He was really concerned about me and the decisions that I had made and was about to make. In this world, relationships are key; who you know is often better than what you know.

In the Bible, Peter asked Jesus if he could come out to him on the water. It was already amazing to see a man, Jesus walking on water, but to ask Him if you can come out there too was just as powerful just to ask. A lot of times we forget the power of asking. God told us that he will give us the desires of our hearts. In so many words, God is asking you, what do me to do for you? Wow, did you get that? Our Heavenly Father is personally asking to do something for us! Now, here is the important part, what do you ask for? Solomon, when asked by God what do you want, he asked for wisdom to lead Gods people effectively. God was so amazed by his request that he gave him all the things that he did not ask for as well. See, what you ask for is just as important as asking.

On my Journey from bouncing back from a life changing past, I finally saw it! I saw myself whole, holy and happy, all at the same time and all by myself. There was no one else there, and I didn't feel that I needed anyone. See, if you remember, loneliness and being alone are 2 separate things; loneliness is a feeling of being alone, whereas being alone is actually a state of believing that you are alone.

When I was going through ONE of my divorces, LOl (it took a long time for me to be able to say that out loud, Thank you Lord for my healing!) now, back to the story. When I was going through one of my divorces, I found myself both lonely and alone. Now, me feeling lonely was true, but me being alone was not true. Again remember, loneliness is a feeling of being alone while being alone is an actual state of being separated, isolated and apart from anyone. Although you may feel alone, you actually are not alone. God has given us a promise that I have learned to appreciate, especially during my tough times and struggles. Deuteronomy 31: 6 reminds us that in the mist of fearful situations, "we are to be strong and courageous, for God will never leave us or forsake us". First of all, I didn't know what being courageous was. I thought it was going on with life without being afraid, but I've learned that it is quite the opposite! It is going on with life even if you are afraid! Wow! What a relief that was for me. I was always afraid of the next step in my life, what am I going to do? Who is going to judge me? How will I respond? Those questions were killing me on the inside. I didn't know if I had the courage to live my life without that someone or something in my life. I thought because I was afraid I was a failure or I was weak. I didn't understand that fear was the very reason why I couldn't get past my past! Fear was destroying me, keeping me hostage to the pain that I was trying so hard to forget, but Oh thank God for courage! Courage is mentioned so many times in the Bible, and now I know why, that word saved my life! Courage taught me that it's okay to be afraid, but it's NOT okay to give in to fear. When I finally learned how to encourage myself, I was able to come up out of my depression, self-pity, doubt, rejection, disappointment, shame and yes, my fear!

I read Jeremiah 29:11 and understood that God had a plan for my life, and it was good and not that sad and disappointing, depressing life I had before. That's when I realized that I may have been lonely, but I definitely was not alone! God was with me the whole entire time, watching over me concerned about my every move. It feels so good to finally breathe again! When I realized that I could really have God promises for my life, and that He was not angry with me, I ask him for one more thing.....a soul mate. Now, understand that I was very afraid to ask Him this question because I had already been married twice before, but I didn't care, I wanted what God said I could have, He said that I can have the desires of my heart, regardless of the mistakes that I have made in my past! I didn't want someone because I was once so broken, I wanted someone because now I am free! Free from all of my past pains that were keeping me from living my best life yet! I was free from depression, rejection, self-pity, pride, doubt, disappointment and yes again, fear! I was free now to love and free to be loved, not to be judged by all of my past mistakes, but to be embraced by all of my new decisions.

I made up in my mine to forgive and to be forgiven, to serve, to worship God freely, to be humble, to help, to love and to pursue happiness in all of its many forms. And, just shortly after my new life journey began, God brought to me the best rib (formerly Tammie Walker, now Tammie Walker Smith) he could create! She is the most fascinating, brilliant, funny, elegant, beautiful, worshiper of God and giver, I have ever known! With already being divorced twice, I thought that my chance of ultimate happiness with someone was over, but I am here to tell you that I am the happiest man I have ever been in my whole entire life! I am so happy, that I don't even remember what my past pains and struggles felt like! Although, I still remember how terrible they were, I just don't remember exactly the painful feelings I had. God has restored all that was broken, lost, stolen or torn. He even restored me from all whom have voluntarily walked out of my life. I am here to tell you that there is Power and Happiness waiting for you on the other side of your pain! Take your New Life Journey NOW, by trusting God, forgiving others, and forgiving yourself. Who knows, today just might be YOUR day!

Chapter Five
In the Wilderness

When I think of wilderness, I focus on its base word "wild". That narrows everything down for me. Before I came to Christ, I was what some people would consider "wild". I didn't do a whole lot, but I did my share. I was brought up in the church, but really wasn't a part of the church. Satan likes us unbalanced and with no sense of direction. That's how he's able to seduce us into his way of thinking. Before you know it, Satan will have you in a wilderness experience. Can you see it, out there all alone in the cold with no one to talk to. Some of you already know what it feels like to be in the wild. You've lost all your family, all your friends, and now all you have is you. You're so confused that you think you're all you need. The problem with thinking that you're all you need is that eventually you start to really believe it.

God saw fit to bless us with the presence of others and we want to run to get away from them. There's power in companionship. As creatures created by the Most High God, we need someone to touch, hold and talk to. You may try to fool yourself into thinking differently, but it won't last long. If, just in case you're successful in your thinking, watch yourself because eventually you'll start talking to toasters, refrigerators, microwaves and possibly yourself. Although that may be common to some, it doesn't have to be that way. In the book of Exodus, the children of Israel found themselves delivered from slavery just to be brought in the wilderness.

With all of the unfamiliarities and insecurities of the wilderness, they found themselves complaining instead of rejoicing. God had heard their cries and had sent a deliverer to their aid, but just because the outcome wasn't what they expected they began to complain. Sound familiar? We always ask God to do something for us, but when He does, we complain because it doesn't turn out the way we expected it to. I remember asking God to give me a closer relationship with Him. Knowing what I had asked for, and knowing what I had to go through to receive it, were two different things. I thought once I asked to be closer to Him, He would allow me to see visions of heaven and the unknown. I thought that while I was sitting at the bus stop, an Angel would appear and talk to me about the things that God wanted me to know or about things that He wanted me to do. But what was all this other stuff I was dealing with? It seemed as if a war was declared on my life. Where did all this stuff come from? My life went from easy street to deep in the valley in a matter of days. I thought God left me for wanting to be closer to Him. It seemed as if Murphy's law only applied to me. Everything that possibly could go wrong in my life went wrong. I found myself suffering more than I ever had before. I was so afraid of not knowing what would happen next that I thought I was going crazy. I would talk to God openly as if I were talking to someone who was physically there. I did it consistently through-out the day, thinking that I was going nuts because I was talking out loud to myself. One morning I was in the bathtub crying, asking God why was this happening to me. He replied; "You said that you wanted to be closer to me". After I heard that, I felt paralyzed. I couldn't speak or move. I just sat there in amazement.

The only way to reach the Father is through His Son Jesus Christ. And to get to know Jesus is to understand His purpose and to experience His suf-ferings. See, the reason why most of us are unable to experience the fullness of God's presence is because most of us don't want to do what is necessary, to suffer for His sake. I know it doesn't feel good to suffer, but once you understand the purpose of suffering, you can begin to embrace the strength that comes from God through suffering. It's no longer about pain, but purpose! It's something that must be done to glorify God. I know some of you may be asking, how does suffering bring glory to God? I'm glad you asked that question.

When you refrain from doing something for yourself for the sake of God, He's pleased. He's pleased because it's something that He didn't have to make you do. You chose to be obedient on your own and if you choose to be obedient on your own then, you're acknowledging your love for Him and his presence. It's like holding on to someone or something you love against their or its will. You keep them trapped because you know that if they could be free, they would leave and never return. But, what if you set them free and they still want to be around you, with no chains attached. They are free to make their own decisions and they decide to stay with you. In that situation, you know that the love is not one-sided. If you keep someone or something trapped because you love him or it, that's not true love because you don't know if that person or thing you have trapped wants to stay with you. So you keep them trapped to make them stay.

I thank God for letting me choose Him on my own. That's the only way to know the difference between real love and fake affections. You notice I didn't say fake love, because I believe either you love someone or something or you don't. Satan traps us not because he loves us, but because he loves to go against the will of God. He gives us things that foolish people believe symbolize love, like fancy houses, cars, jewelry, clothes, money, an unequally yoked mate, and a job that hinders God's will for your life. All these things and more if given may seem like the giver loves you, but don't be deceived. God gives us something greater............chastisement. Chastisement!!! Yes. How can whipping us be greater? He whips us for doing wrong so we don't stray away from His truth. God loves us and He doesn't want to see us perish. Satan doesn't care if we do wrong or not. He doesn't care if we perish. As a matter of fact, he wants us to perish. So, what he has to offer is just the bait to eternal damnation! If you have something or someone trapped and you want to know if its true love, set them free. Love is not forced, it's embraced. It should be their decision on whether to leave or stay. If you happen to find yourself in a wilderness experience, afraid and all alone, be strong and don't lose hope. You're only passing through.

Chapter Six
Waiting 4 back up!

I'm instantly reminded of the time when I was about 11 years old. I remember playing with friends in the park where we lived. We were rudely interrupted by other kids from another neighborhood. Nothing was strange about that because we always shared the park. But, this particular day, I was swinging on the swing when one particular boy tried to force me out of my swing. He grabbed my swing and tried to push me out. He wasn't bigger than I was, he just had a lot of brothers. So, being the person that I was,

I was going to let him have the swing, until one of my friends grabbed him and pushed him to the ground. He held him there and told me to kick him! Everyone began shouting kick him, kick him! It got so bad that my friends began kicking him because I wouldn't. There was nothing he could do, but just lie there on the ground and get kicked. I told them I was going to kick him and to let him up. Needless to say, they didn't listen to me until someone shouted and said, "here come his brothers"! Everyone ran, including me! Nothing further happened in that matter, but it sparked something in me that felt good. I said to myself, it sure was good they came when they did. I was fascinated with the idea that someone came to his aid, just in time. Whether we want to believe it or not, God is just like that. He will always rescue us from the grip of Satan and ourselves. The only problem is how long do we have to stay held down before He comes? Just like the young man, the children of Israel practiced being rebellious.

And every time they needed to be bailed out of a terrible situation, God was always there. They worshipped false gods and did things that God told them not to do, but they still had the nerve to call on Him when they needed to be delivered. Whether you believe this or not, God gets tired of the same old thang(thing). You say you're going to be good, but you end up doing bad. And this has become a cycle in your life. Say good things, but do bad things, say good things, but do bad things, say good things, but do bad things. You get the picture. We fail to realize that when we react in disobedience to God, we are pushed further and further away from His presence and from our blessings. The more we sin, the further we are pushed away.

Some of us have been sinning for so long that we can't even find God. He seems to be totally absent from our lives. That's when it's tough because when you're down and discouraged, you feel held down and no one comes to rescue you because you don't know who to call for help. It seems like you're yelling for help, but no one hears you. Satan is kicking you and he's got all of his demons kicking you to. Satan is so sneaky, that when you're down, he will have you kicking yourself. He won't need anyone else to do his dirty work because you'll be doing it for him.

Listen to me, I know what I'm talking about. You're listening to someone who graduated from the karate school of "kicking yourself when you're down" technology center. Most of the time, we're our own worst enemies.

The mind is so powerful that it makes things exist whether they exist or not. That's why Satan attacks your mind first because the mind controls everything else. The mind is the battlefield between God and Satan. The Bible says to not be conformed to the ways of the world, but be ye transformed by the renewing of your _____?…..........mind. You know it's really simple. If you stop thinking the way Satan wants you to think, you can start thinking your way out of your present situation. The Father wants us to know that we have a big brother and His name is Jesus. You will never have to go through this life alone anymore. Isn't that wonderful! I know there is someone in need of help right now as he or she read these words. I'm here to tell you that if you call on Jesus like you really need him, He will come running to rescue you in your time of need. He will be right there, to back you up.

Chapter Seven
Don't want to be Alone

One of the biggest problems that people have today is the thought of being alone. We fear the idea of living a lifestyle of being alone. Where did this fear come from? Why do we allow it to overcome us? Well, first of all we know that fear doesn't come from God. Second, fear hinders growth. I remember when I first learned to swim. All my friends were advanced swimmers and I was still wet behind the ears, so to speak. It wasn't the fact that they were better swimmers, they were just not afraid of putting their heads under the water. In fact, when they did try to swim they would only stay in the same spot. But that's not the issue, the issue is that they had mastered the fear of drowning. Now, because they had mastered that fear, they were able to move ahead and progress in the art of swimming. Whereas I, on the other hand, was hindered in my growth in learning how to swim because of my fear of drowning. I don't care what aspect in life you place it in, whether marriage, business, job or education, whatever it is, you will not move forward in anything if you're afraid of what may happen. Can't you see the hooks of the devil? He shows us things that may go wrong so we won't move out into that unfamiliar ground. As long as he can make you think in advance that the move that you're about to make in life could fail, you will not make the move. Although the move that you didn't make could have been the break you were looking for, but you will never know because you were too afraid to try. Life is like the game of chess. We are set up on earth in a plan made for us to win and succeed in life. Satan is our opponent who is also set up on earth in a plan made for him to win and succeed in defeating us. See, before you were born, God knew what you would and could be. So, He placed you where you would be greatly used in order to overcome the opposition of Satan. Some of us are leaders, so he places us out front. Others are soldiers, helpers, operators and even on lookers. So, He places us where we're needed.

When we make a move in life toward our winning destination, guess what? Satan, makes a move also to stop us. For every move we make, Satan makes one also. We must always be ready and watchful of the moves Satan makes because he's cunning and skillful. And if we're not careful, he will take one of our soldiers and place himself closer within our realm. Unfortunately, this is more than just a game. Satan wants more than to just take us out of the game and set us aside, he wants to destroy us completely. He wants us out of the game forever! But glory be to God that the game has been rigged for us to win regardless of the moves Satan makes. Satan is outnumbered three to one, by the Father, the Son and the Holy Spirit. They're all working twenty four hours a day to prevent us from making the wrong moves. And if we listen and obey their commands, we will finish this race victorious. But, and I don't like buts, if we move on our own, not listening for instructions, we will find ourselves caught behind enemy lines destined to be destroyed. We shouldn't move out alone, without the guidance of the Holy Spirit. That's one of the reasons why being alone is so detrimental. The thought of being alone is so horrific that God made someone (Eve) just so Adam would have someone to be with. I could just imagine what it would be like if God had not created Eve. Some of us would have horse heads and duck legs or zebra bodies with human hands. Ladies, can you imagine having a giraffe head with ostrich legs? How are you going to put on stockings with pumps with ostrich feet? Or, men can you imagine having a gorilla face with an elephant tail? How are we going to put on a nice pair of slacks with a tail like that? I don't know, just my crazy imagination. Thank God for Eve!

But, back to the subject at hand. After my divorce, I practiced abstinence for about three years. I had no sex, no kisses, no relationship, no nothing. To you who are probably saying like my friends did, you had no life, you are quite wrong. As strange as it may seem, on the contrary, I had more life than I had ever had before. Not because I was thrilled about being a bachelor, but because I learned to be by myself, but not alone. I went out by myself one time and the lady asked if I was alone. I said no, she said, but no one is with you. I said, physically no one is with me, but spiritually someone is always with me. She smiled, and went on. Some of you may think that's too religious, but let me tell you something; it's real.

We need to understand that we may be by ourselves at some point in our lives, but we are not alone. When I grasped this concept, I felt like a chick that had just hatched from its egg. I felt so alive! I remember talking to God out loud as if someone were physically there. I began having conversations with Him out loud. Again, I thought I was going out of my mind, but this craziness brought me so much peace and gave me so much strength! I continued my relationship with God in this manner because I liked the way it made me feel. When normally I wouldn't make a move unless someone was with me or unless someone agreed with me, I found myself moving out on my own, with the help of God. Not alone, just by myself. No one wants to be alone. That's why we make bad decisions in relationships, because of that fear of being without. So we would be with anyone as long as he or she was breathing. Ouch! That hurt! Did anyone feel that! A lot of people are with someone, but still feel alone. If you still feel alone with someone there, why are you carrying that dead weight along with you? If you're going to have someone with you, at least make sure that they know that they're with you. God told us that "He will never leave us nor forsake us". There is no guessing or wondering if He's there, He is! And until you grasp that concept, you will always be alone.

So, don't just settle for people who come and go in your life. Put your trust in God, someone who will be there when everyone else is gone, waiting, willing and ready.

Chapter Eight
Timing Is Everything

Genesis chapter 1 verse 1 says, "Let there be light". This was the beginning of time as we know it, or was it? Have you ever thought of time before there ever was a beginning? And if there was time, what was its purpose before the beginning? Is time a person referred to as father time? Does God wear a Timex? How does time affect us? I don't know. Yes. I don't know. Definitely not. Don't think so. Let's see.

When I was younger, much younger, time seemed so long compared to now and I'm only 34.

It seemed as if the sun stayed out for about two months and then began to set. Now, it seems as if it rises and sets in two hours. God's existence doesn't revolve around time, time revolves around God. Time comes before God and says, "when do I do what you desire for me to do". That's amazing! I'm not implying that time is a person, but only that God and only God has control of time. This is the very reason why each day of life is so important. We don't know when it will be over. For some, it's already over, but for others it's just beginning. So, each minute of time, should be used with extreme caution.

We should not think that time is something to waste, because it was not created as a waste. It was created as a systematic chronological measure of things to come. We were born, we live and we die. Jesus was born, He lived, He died, but He was resurrected and He will come again. This will happen in due time. A lot of people have missed out on important blessings because of this misunderstanding of time. I'm a person that likes to take life by the horns and jump at opportunities, but sometimes I move too fast. And when that happens, the door that God was preparing to open is closed due to my lack of understanding of timing. Some move to fast, others move too slow. Understand, you can't control time, only God controls time. He knows what doors to open when they're ready to be opened. He also knows what doors to close when they're ready to be closed. I'm not telling you to just sit back and wait for things to happen, I'm telling you not to force things to happen. Time is not something to be forced, it's something to be embraced. Often, people force us to do something in a certain allotted time. If we find ourselves coming short of completing this task in the time required, we become stressed. Our bodies tense up, our brain cells start to run out of our heads and we look for the closest bridge to jump from. The best thing to do when you find yourself coming up short of completing a task in its required time, is to say, "I'm not going to worry about something that I cannot control." A lot of us try to cram a whole lifetime of events in eight hours. That's impossible for us to do! It makes no sense to go through life stressed and worried over something you have no control over. We must learn to give our troubles to God because He loves us and He also controls what we can't.......time.

I remember receiving a cut off notice on my utility bill. They gave me five days to get the money. It would take me two weeks to have enough money to cover the bill. I tried everything I knew how to come up with the money, but came up short. With the little money I had, I went to the grocery store and bought some candles because the deadline was near. When I got home I placed the candles on the table and sat and stared at them. After staring at those candles for a while, I began to pray. I asked God to let His will be done and if He wanted my lights to be off, then let them be off, but if not, to make a way for them to stay on. On the morning of the last day, I called the utility office and talked with someone in customer service. She connected me to someone in billing who connected me to someone else. When I finally reached the the right person to talk to, I explained my situation to her. She was extremely helpful and granted me more time to pay based upon my agreement to pay by the date we agreed upon. My utilities stayed on and my faith was increased. Most of us face greater tragedies than that of a utility bill. Many times we look for God to bless us one way and He chooses to bless us another way. However the blessing may come, thank God it came. We never know what angle He's coming from, we just have to be faithful and ready. We can't be impatient and give up, we must allow God time to prove Himself to us. Most of us don't see the hand of God moving in our life because we don't give God's hand a chance to move. We ask God for something and just when He's about to answer, we jump up and try to do it ourselves. Sounds like who? We must be patient and allow God time to answer our prayers. He's not going anywhere, so there's no need to rush Him.

Most of our problems stem from being impatient. Some of us married the wrong person because we either couldn't wait to have sex or because our biological clocks were ticking. Well, guess what? Now, that you've gotten yourself in a big mess and it feels like you're living in hell, your biological clock is still ticking. I can't express how important it is to wait on God to choose your mate. Some of us, instead of jumping the broom, we've jumped right into the fire and have been burning ever since. All marriages are not ordained by God. And when you find out that you're with someone else's husband or wife, that's no excuse for divorce. The best thing to do is to bring your marriage before God like you did at first at the altar, and confess your wrong doings and ask God to bless your marriage. Just because he or she is not your soul mate doesn't mean that your marriage still can't be beautiful. Learn to wait on God for the provisions of your life. Rushing into anything is not a good thing. Take time out and consult with God. Then wait for His reply.

Some of you are probably asking, well, how do I know when the time is right? I'm glad you asked that question. Seek God and keep knocking. If the door opens and the timing is right, go inside.

Chapter Nine
911

Heart pounding, nervous, anxious, unfo-
cused, having difficulty breathing, can't
think, lost. Ever felt that way before? I have. This
feeling or state of emergency has occurred at least
two to three times in a person's life. Do you remember what it was that made you feel this way last?
How did you respond? Where you able to overcome
the feeling enough to do what was needed to make
it better? Or, are you one of those individuals that
are able to remain calm despite the circumstances?
Contrary to popular belief, there are people who

have the ability to remain calm in situations that would bring other people literally to their knees. Some say that these people are not in touch with their emotions. Others say they just don't care about anything or that they've never truly been through any real life emergency situation. Isn't that just like us to ridicule someone just because they don't react like the norm. Maybe it's the other way around. Maybe these individuals have been through many emergency situations which have given them the knowledge of self-control. They've learned to control their emotions, giving them the strength to solve the situation with tact because they've learned that panicking is not the way to react in an emergency situation.

There are always two sides to anything, but only one can be correct or true. I'm reminded of an incident that occurred with a four year old girl. The little girl had a fever of 104 which was rising. When the parents were unable to bring the fever down, the little girl began to a have a seizure. Now we know that this was a very critical moment for this little girl and her parents. During the seizure, the father asked the mother to go and call 911. The mother ran down the hall, then returned to the room and asked, "what's the number"? Although now it may be funny when they go back and think about it, but at the time it wasn't. In emergency situations, you are tested on what you know, not what you think. Oh, by the way, the little girl I've mentioned is healthy, doing fine and getting on her parents' nerves. But what if no one had really known what to do? If that was the case, then this would not be such a good report.

All of our lives, we have been drilled on what to do in an emergency situation. They have classes, seminars, books, video tapes, cassette tapes, conferences, stickers, magazines, pamphlets and commercials. You want it, they've got it! They do all these things so that you will know what to do. Now, could someone please explain to me like I'm a four year old why we know how to call everyone else in an emergency situation, but God? The message has been lost. We need to drill into our children to call on God first and then, if needed, to call for emergency assistance. We're in the habit of calling everyone else first and if they don't come through, we call on God. There's no wonder why He is withholding His blessings from us. I could imagine God being both mad and jealous. First, mad because we put others before Him. And second, jealous because we believed that man could solve our problems better than He. If you call God first, you may not need anyone else second. I use the word "may" because the decision is God's what He wants to do in your situation.

There are many, many, many, miraculous testimonies of God's power showing through in times of need. But I'm referring to day to day struggles when you feel like you need help now! We can't always neglect God in our lives, He loves us too much for us to do that to Him. Everyday we're being taught and trained on what to do. It's time to renew our minds. We need to call on God everyday. Converse with him about your needs as well as your wants. I remember when I was struggling with some hard times in my life and I called on friends and family and no one could help me. When I got tired of asking for help from friends and family, I began to talk to God and He gave me understanding and strength to endure my pain. We must learn to call on God first in times of need, because it's not guaranteed that when you call on man he will be available to help you.

I'm reminded in the bible book of I kings 18th chapter, about the four hundred and fifty prophets who called on their god. The agreement was to prepare a bull and place it upon wood to be burned. But the fire must come from the true God. So, the four hundred and fifty prophets called out to their god Baal to rain down fire to burn the wood. They cried out to Baal from morning to evening and nothing happened. Would you want to serve a god like this? You're in a serious situation and he's gone out to lunch. But Elisha on the other hand called out to the one and only true God. And not only did He burn up the bull, but He burned the wood and the ground that was around the altar and even dried up the water that was in the ditch! That's what I'm talking about! That's the God that I want on my side!

If you're ever going to be in an emergency situation like I know you will, there's no other God like the Father, the Son and the Holy Spirit. Got a 911 situation? Call Him, then stand back!!!

Chapter Ten
Are You Sure

Doesn't it feel great to have the power of knowledge? When I was growing up, all the older people were telling me to stay in school because knowledge is power. Is that the reason why we try to learn so much? What happened to understanding? I know people and you may know some also, who want to know everything just so that they can tell you what you don't know. We love to put ourselves on super tall pedestals, so that others may see our accomplishments. Some people would go into a Super-Duper cardiac arrest (heart attack), if you took all of their educational degrees or accomplishments away from them. It's sad when all we live for is to see how successful we can become. A person who chases success is like a sail boat guided by the wind. That person doesn't know where to go, he will just go where he is pushed. If he thinks he will be successful in the valley, he will go in the valley. If he thinks he will be successful in the mountains, guess what, he'll go to the mountains. Whatever and wherever it is, it doesn't matter as long as there is an opportunity of being successful.

I used to wonder what it meant to be successful. Then, through my sufferings, I found the answer. Success is not accomplishing what you set out to do, that's selfishness. Success is when you set out and accomplish what God wants you to do. Most of us feel because we've gained more than others, whether materially or mentally, we are greater than they. It's o.k. to improve ourselves and to push for things that we desire. But before you begin to push, make sure what you're pushing for is what God wants you to push for. Sometimes, we push too hard and too far and push ourselves right out of the will of God. Trust me when I tell you this. I know by experience, the perfect teacher.

I used to be a person who operated by my written things to do list. If anything stopped me from doing those things, my life was messed up. I believed in order. I believed that if you organized your steps to accomplish a certain task, your chances to succeed would be greater. There is nothing wrong with that thought, but what happens when everything doesn't work out the way you planned it? Do you shut down and start all back over or do you pick up the pieces and keep pushing? Some of us can't deal with the unknown, that's why our life must be the way we want it or we will literally a have a nervous breakdown. We must understand that we're here to do a specific work, not the work of ourselves. We're not to go about our own personal agendas, unless they have been approved by God.

You see, that person who chases success might have his priorities mixed up, but there is one thing about that person that we all could learn from, and that's the ability to be flexible. Learn to operate in any state of mind. In this life, things hardly ever go the way we plan them. So, we must be prepared to accept the experience and regroup, and keep on going. A sailboat is concerned with only one thing, its destination. It may be pushed by the wind from one side of the sea to the other, but its purpose is to stay on course and make it to its destination.

As Christians, we must not be so driven to give up if things don't work out the way we like. I was led by God to do a number of things that, to me and others, showed no sign or evidence of being prosperous. Then, I began to wonder was it really God who spoke to me. Satan's most powerful weapon is the tool of deception. He makes us second guess or feel unsure about the things we know were given to us by God. Just like Eve in the garden of Eden, we are persuaded to think the thoughts that are implanted into our minds by Satan. Eve knew that the tree was forbidden, but because Satan used words that altered her thinking, she took a bite of the bait and was hooked into being disobedient to God. Isn't that amazing that sin begins with a thought? Satan knows that if he controls your thoughts, he controls you. The problem with that is that he knows that and we don't.

The mind is the battlefield. What you think determines your destiny! You can go where your mind takes you or better than that, you can be what your mind perceives you to be. Did Jesus not tell the woman who had been sick for twelve years that it was her faith that healed her in the bible book of Matthew 9: 20-22? What if we start believing that we have peace or wisdom or strength or money or land or ministries that really help people or watch out, Godly sent wives or husbands? Wouldn't that be awesome! Guess what? It can happen, if only you believe!

Speaking of Godly sent wives and husbands. When God sends that man or woman you've prayed for, don't allow Satan to use his words to control your thoughts into thinking anything different. God has brought Godly husbands and wives to people and just because one thing doesn't "click", we think that person is not from God. Maybe God brought him or her because He knew it wouldn't click just to make you tick and start acting right. And once you tick and act right, your mate will begin to tick also and then everything will begin to click together for Him. Remember there's not one person on this earth that is perfect. The perfect person "Jesus" was already on earth, but now He is in Heaven. Your God given spouse may not be perfect, but if God gave him to you, he is perfect for you.

See, God puts us with people who we can help or they can help us. I know you don't want to hear that because you do everything right. Wrong! You may be the upstanding Christian, you read the

Bible more than once a day, you pray for everyone, you visit the sick and shut-ins, you feed the hungry and you teach Sunday school class. All these things are wonderful and continue to do them, but if you are bitter, jealous, envious, deceitful, a liar, self-centered, prideful, lazy and many other things too many to mention, you can stand to be improved.

Most of the time we think that the things that our spouses do that tick us off show the stupidity and imperfections of our spouse. Well, are you ready for this? God will unite you with someone who seem to be below average, just to show you that you're below average. We're too busy pointing out the faults of others, when God will use the faults of others to reveal the faults of ourselves. Maybe the fact that your spouse makes you angry all the time is a sure sign that you need to work on that fruit of the Spirit self-control. Those who have the most spiritual strength must lead by example. Don't rush the growth of your spouse. He is not perfect and neither are you. Spend quality time with your spouse's spiritual growth. Ask and answer questions he may have and don't make him feel stupid if he doesn't know the correct answer.

In a world unsure of its beliefs, there is one thing that we do know, that we have Blessed Assurance in Jesus Christ.

Chapter Eleven
Finding Your Center

The definition of the word center is a point about which something turns. The way in which we interpret center is not, I believe, the way God interprets it. I'm not saying that God doesn't want our lives to revolve around Him because He does. But there is another side to that coin. If you remember, in the beginning, everything was perfect, even Adam, God's first created man. The garden of Eden was where God placed Adam and there was balance. Everything did exactly what it was created to do in this grand scheme of things, because they had a place and they knew it. But before anything can be balanced, it must be centered. For example, if you try to hang a picture on a wall, you want to make sure the nail is nailed in the center of the area in the wall in which you want to hang the picture. In order to do so, you measure the wall so that it will have equal lengths on each side of the nail. Once you've found your center, you implant your nail, hang your picture and then balance it. Our lives are very similar to that picture. We're waiting around for someone to place us where we're supposed to be. The problem with that is if we aren't careful, people will put us where they want us to be. Then, we'll go through life fulfilling someone else's purpose and not God's. (ouch, that hurt!). To avoid such a catastrophe, we must search and find our center. But, let me tell you. You will not be able to find your center unless God is the center of your life.

Some of us are in places or situations because we've allowed someone else to place us where they wanted us to be. Or perhaps we were too impatient to give God the time that was needed to balance us. On a scale, weight is distributed equally to both sides to create a straight plane. The definition of the word balance is an adjustment in order to bring about proportion; evenness of mind and emotions; equilibrium and steadiness.

Let's take the example of the picture. First, location must be identified. This decision is not yours, it's Gods'. This can also be associated with purpose: why are you here, what are you supposed to do and where are you supposed to go? Second, the center is found for nailing. This decision is yours. Our center is Jesus. The center is the foundation on which the purpose is fulfilled. He should be first in <u>All</u> things and <u>All</u> things should revolve around Him. Last is balance. This belongs to both you and God. Weight <u>will</u> be distributed to both sides whether you like it or not, but it is up to you to find and maintain the strength needed to uphold it. In life, weight will be distributed not only to both sides of your life like that of a scale, but to every side of your life. You will receive large parts of weight in areas that you may feel are weak and smaller portions in those areas that you may feel are strong. To you, this makes no sense because you seem off balance. But to God, who is our center, knows best. He knows how to adjust us in the way where we will receive balance. You see, it makes no sense to place greater volumes or to place greater tests upon you in areas where you are strong. The enemy Satan will not try to overtake you where you are strong, he will always come to your weak side. For example, if your weak side is money, guess what, he will attack the area in which you receive your money. If your weak side is your spouse, he will definitely attack your spouse. This is why we must always pray for our spouses because they are the closest to us. If your weak side is faith, Satan will try to give you reasons to doubt God. God tries to keep us balanced, by placing those things in our lives that we feel we can't handle. He knows what areas in our lives need to be strengthened. Isn't that awesome! I know most of us feel as if we know what's best, but in reality we really don't. If we did, we would not have suffered so greatly in our pasts. Some of us are still suffering because we have not allowed or refuse to allow, God the opportunity to balance us.

Life will not begin to show completeness until we yield to our creator, the One responsible for giving us purpose. And without that knowledge of our individual purpose, we will continue to roam this earth as dust in the wind, not knowing where we will end up. Be still, and allow God to balance you.

Chapter Twelve
Damaged Goods

When I was about 18 years old, I used to work in a grocery store not far from where I lived. I was responsible for cleaning the floors and sometimes stocking the shelves. I worked on the graveyard shift. The graveyard shift was the time when all the store preparations were done. I never knew why it was called the graveyard shift until I started working at the grocery store. It's called the graveyard shift because that's the time when you should be dead asleep instead of awake working. It took a lot of getting used to on that

shift. My first night I was caught sleeping on a pal-
let of potatoes in the storeroom. Luckily, my friend
was the manager at that time, who only laughed at
me for being asleep.

When I got over sleeping on the job, I worked
sometimes stocking shelves as I mentioned earlier.
To my surprise, I saw something that was quite
disturbing. When we were opening boxes of
food items, we sometimes made a mistake and
cut the individual boxes inside in a way that was
not presentable for sale. So, when that happened
we were asked to put those items aside. This
procedure was something that I understood, but
what I witnessed later was something that I didn't
understand.

Each night a person was picked to gather all
the damaged goods together and take them to the
back warehouse. On one particular night, I was
picked to collect all the damaged goods. When
I gathered them all together, I took them to the
warehouse as I was told. When I got there, I didn't

see any place designated for damaged goods. I saw places designated for incoming goods, outgoing goods, new orders, ordered items, etc., but nothing for damaged goods. Not wanting to feel stupid, I left them in the baskets together in a section of the warehouse. I was sure they had a place, but I just didn't know where. In the morning when the managers did their inspection, they noticed the baskets left in the warehouse. Bringing it to my attention they asked, "why didn't you put the damaged goods away?" I responded, "I did". I told them that I was told to put them in the warehouse, but I didn't see a place for them so I made one. Laughing at me again, they told me to follow them to the warehouse so that I might be shown where these items went. When we arrived, each manager grabbed a food item out of the baskets and said, "here is where they go". One by one they begin throwing the damaged goods in the dumpster. Shocked and surprised I shouted, "what are you doing?" I began thinking about all the people who are without food and they were throwing away good food. The food item's label may be torn or the box cut open, but the food inside is still good. They told me to chill out. That means relax for those of you who are not from the hood. They said these items could not be sold or given away because of the risk involved. Once the food items are open, they're exposed. I was told that insurance companies are very strict about the presentation of food items. I could understand that from a business point of view, but I was still disturbed. Here we have people starving every day and yet we throw away good food. I don't work at the grocery store anymore, but that incident really impacted my life. To this day I'm very mindful of wasting things. I don't even like to see things being wasted by others.

As I go back and reflect the past, I'm so grateful God doesn't waste things. If we're honest with ourselves, most of us, if not all, would acknowledge the fact that we too are or were damaged goods. A rip here or there, torn, cut, bent and bruised, we've been there. I don't know about you, but many times I felt as if I was no use to anyone or even God because of the hardships I've encountered. Some of us have experienced the loss of a loved one, been molested, raped, battered, addicted to drugs or alcohol, homeless and even left for dead. We've been divorced, cheated on, lied on, talked about, mislead and even forgotten about. With the things we've encountered, we're sometimes made to feel useless. We feel very unsure of ourselves, our future and even God. We don't even care about the way we look sometimes, just going from day to day. When we feel this way, we feel we're only good for whomever and whatever anyone will use us for. WOW! THANK YOU JESUS! When I think about this, I'm encouraged even more because if I'm only good for whatever anyone will use me for, then I'm more than what I think I am. Follow me. Because when others misused and abused me, they had no use for me, but God said he would accept me just as I am. He doesn't care if I'm bent or bruised, torn or ripped, cut or broken. He doesn't care, all He wants is me! HALLELUIA! The world may try to make you feel useless, but you tell the world that you are being used by God. The pains that we once had or have were and are real, but we're not going to let our pains dictate to us who we are. The enemy Satan loves to keep those pains fresh in your mind so that you may feel those disturbing emotions all over again, throwing you off track. But when he bring those disturbing thoughts to your mind via television, radio, internet, conversation, books, etc., you bind that devil and those thoughts in the mighty name of JESUS! I MEAN IT! I want you to say, "THOUGHTS OF DESTRUCTION, GET OUT OF MY MIND IN THE MIGHTY NAME OF JESUS!" Then, start thinking about something else. Go and eat some chicken, go and get in the car, go and take a shower, I don't know, but do something other than think those thoughts. I'm coming to you right now in the mighty name of our Lord and Savior Jesus. You are healed and no longer a damaged good. God wants to use you right now. Don't ever let anyone or anything make you feel less that what you really are. The enemy Satan is trying very hard to throw you away, but he's so stupid he doesn't know that God uses everything He creates. So, wipe those tears away and tell yourself that you are worth something because Jesus paid a high price for you. You may not realize it, but you're expensive. And God keeps all of His valuable things in a safe place, in His Will.

Chapter Thirteen
Starting Over

Walking down the sidewalk, blue skies above, fall leaves falling from the trees with a touch of a gentle breeze. Feels good doesn't it? Not a care in the world. Do you remember the last time you felt this way? If you do, what's the difference in your life now than then? I don't want to say that whatever changes were made were bad choices, but I do want you to evaluate them. Most of our sorrows derive from bad choices. Whether it be finances, jobs, homes, cars, spouses and even whom we worship. A friend once told me that if he could go back in time, his life would be much better. Maybe so, but I also have to believe that there would still be new mistakes made. Bad choices may be made, but you will improve as long as you learn from them. If you don't learn from them, you may find them very hard to live with. Some chose to follow Christ because they thought it would make their lives easier. We can't go through this life without feeling the pains of Christianity. We may want to, but we can't. Being children of the almighty God and brothers and sisters of our Lord and Savior Jesus Christ, we must bear the same burdens even if that means being without. "For what will it profit a man to gain the whole world and lose his soul" Matthews 16:26. Most of us believe that the key to happiness is what we have materially. I won't lie to you, it feels good to enjoy the finer things offered by God. But what if we never get that opportunity? Will you lead a life of misery or will you re-evaluate your purpose for living? We were not created to enjoy material things, but material things were created for us to enjoy. We as believers are in a season of demanded obedience. In order to receive anything from God, we must obey Him fully. We must follow His commands and praise and worship Him daily. If we want change, we must do something different! We as husbands and fathers must rise to the responsibilities of our families and lead with a firm, but gentle hand. And wives and mothers must also rise to that same responsibility to their families while supporting the responsibilities of their husbands. This is not the time for any of us to become jealous of one another. Know your place in God and in your family. There is a divine order, and it is and will be regardless of the way you feel. God honors families that respect Him in worship because of its' ability to produce fruit. "Every tree that doesn't bear fruit will be cut down" Matthew 3:10. When a family member loses his connection to the family through disobedience, he becomes exposed. He has chosen to not follow the divine order of God. So now through disobedience, the enemy Satan has greater opportunities to destroy him. Because you decided to disobey the divine order, you may have lost any chance of personal future blessings. It may have been your future finances, healing, deliverance, peace, understanding, joy and even wisdom, that you forfeited. And for what? Whatever it was that you chose. I hope whatever you chose was worth it, because Satan is waiting for that perfect opportunity for you to be exposed, out from under the protection of God so that he can destroy you. When we disobey God, we come out from under His protection. And that's not a safe place to be. When we look back over our lives, it should be easy for us to see God's mercy. God has continued to protect and provide for us all these years regardless of how much we've disappointed Him. So, what can we do to show our appreciation? Change. We must change our ways and our lifestyles for Him. In the past we were drug users, alcoholics, abusers, misusers, liars, cheaters, adulterers, fornicators and much, much more. But now is the time to change. We must come out of ourselves and let God condition and fashion us to His will. Don't dwell any longer on what used to be or what could have been. Now is the time to think about what's going to be, a new you! A person full of God's Spirit! Enabled to conquer things that were once thought to be impossible. Your focus will be less on you and more on God. Allow God's mind to enter yours so that it may be renewed. It's true, you may still feel the blows of the enemy, but they will not defeat you. You may even fall, but you will rise again! And one thing is for sure; you will not be the same again. God is now giving you a brand new opportunity to start over. Repent all of your sins to God and be cleansed. It's time for you to rejoice and be happy. It's time for you to receive what is rightfully yours, your freedom. Not freedom to do wrong, but freedom to praise and worship God as you truly desire, with love. So, let your world come crashing down all around you, it's o.k. because you can't do anything about it anyway. Jesus said He has conquered the world and if we accepted Jesus, that means we are conquerors to.

I pray that you will accept this new opportunity to change and to start all over again, because you may not get a second chance. Embrace the future that awaits you with many many blessings in store, in Jesus' name, Amen.

Chapter Fourteen
What Happens Now?

Well, what does happen now? Do you go back to the way things were or do you make a change? You know, one thing that really amazes me is how we know what our problems are, but we're too afraid or too weak to fix them. It's one thing to be in a situation beyond your control, but it's another thing to be in a situation that you can control and still in it. Let's stop making excuses and start facing our problems. Yes I know it's hard and I know it hurts, but you can't continue to stay where you are. Where you are right now is not where you want to be and you know it. If you want things to change, you have to start doing something different. I know you feel left out, not loved, afraid and out of control. But there's more to life than what you feel. You can't let the way you feel control your future. If you let that happen, you will be up and down for the rest of your life. So what, your marriage is failing, your job is not fulfilling, your children are leaving and your health is not at its best. Let me tell you something, in the midst of all of your worries lies an unbelievable peace. Yes, it's true. It comes from God our Father and lies right within you. But the problem is that you don't realize it. Or maybe you do realize it, but you're too burden down for it to surface. That's my concern. That's the reason why you can't go back to the way things were. So, say farewell. Say farewell to the bad marriage, the guilt that you held on to over a loved one that passed, the lost job, the repossessed car, the foreclosed home, the bad doctor's report, the bad choices, the lack of money, the low self esteem and all the negative thoughts that the devil gave you. Now is the time to make a change! First, we're going to change our thoughts to think nothing but good. Regardless of the way we feel, we're going to think only on what is good in our life. Your life may be turned upside down, but there is something that is good in your life. Focus on that. Second, we're going to be like the Nike sneakers and just do it! Do what you may ask? Do--it! Start something new. Start a new relationship with God, get a new car, look at a new house, put an extra $5.00 in the collection plate at church, make new friends, start your own business, start exercising, start treating yourself, find a new man or woman if you're not married and if you are, pray that God will start something new in them. I'm just trying to get you to see that if you continue to do the same things, you will continue to get the same results. Look back over your life, year after year it's the same old thang and nothing has changed. This has got to stop! I'm going to say it one more time, if you want change you have to do something different. If you normally go left, start going right. If you use to give a little, start giving a lot. You will be amazed to know that a small change could have a great impact. I do something that I like to call "hug therapy". I try to hug at least three to five people a day. Not just a physical bump accompanied with a pat on the back. I'm talking about a real hug, filled with love, compassion and genuine concern. Do you know what that could do for someone who is silently struggling with problems too difficult to handle? It could change their whole life! And from what you may think is nothing….a hug. I plead with you to don't just go back to the way things were. Make up in your mind that you want things to be different, then do it. God is with you. Set goals and be strong. It may get tough, but don't make excuses. Trust God, because that's the only way you'll win.

Conclusion & Dedication

As we look back over our lives we see many mistakes made, but no changes in making sure those same mistakes don't come back to haunt us. I'm almost sure in believing that no one enjoys the pain of bad choices. So, why do we keep making them? Is it because we don't know better or is it because were too stubborn to learn? I've made many mistakes not listening to God, and I got tired of being tossed around like a sailboat without a captain. I needed to know the course that was outlined for my life and I needed to know now. So, I started seeking the One responsible for creating me, God. God showed me what my purpose was and He forgave me for all the dumb choices I had made. Now, I have a second chance to get it right, not for my sake, but so that others may have a second chance also and know that He is God. Sure it gets hard sometimes, but as long as I'm guided by His presence, I won't get lost. He will make absolutely sure that I'm taken care of and that His will for my life will be fulfilled. And on top of all of that, He told me just because I chose to believe in Him, whatever I desire to have He will give it to me. You can't beat that deal. If you want your situation to change, you have to do something different!

Acknowledgements

To my parents Charlie and Ola Smith,

Although you were physically unable to hear and speak, you still heard my cries and spoke strength into my life. I thank God for your lives.

Lord, I dedicate this writing to you. For all You've done for me. I wanted to write all the things You've done for me in this section, but I would need all the paper in the universe to complete this. I know You already know the way I feel, but that's what I wanted to do. Anyway, I miss You and I can't wait to see Your face. So until then, take care of my parents and let them know that I miss them greatly.

Love, Your son Andrews